RAISING THE FLAG

THE BATTLE OF IWO JIMA

BY TERRI DOUGHERTY

CONSULTANT:
Tim Solie
Adjunct Professor of History
Minnesota State University, Mankato

Capstone
press
Mankato, Minnesota

Edge Books are published by Capstone Press,
151 Good Counsel Drive, P.O. Box 669, Mankato, Minnesota 56002.
www.capstonepress.com

Library of Congress Cataloging-in-Publication Data
Dougherty, Terri.
    Raising the flag: the Battle of Iwo Jima / by Terri Dougherty.
    p. cm. — (Edge books. Bloodiest battles.)
    Summary: "Describes events before, during, and after the Battle of Iwo Jima,
including key players, weapons, and battle tactics" — Provided by publisher.
    Includes bibliographical references and index.
    ISBN-13: 978-1-4296-1939-4 (hardcover)
    ISBN-10: 1-4296-1939-2 (hardcover)
    1. Iwo Jima, Battle of, Japan, 1945 — Juvenile literature. I. Title. II. Series.
D767.99.I9D68 2009
940.54'2528 — dc22   2008000528

Editorial Credits
Mandy Robbins, editor; Bob Lentz, designer/illustrator; Jo Miller,
    photo researcher

Photo Credits
AP Images/Joe Rosenthal, cover (bottom); Louis R. Lowery, 22; Max Desfor, 8
Corbis/Swim Ink 2, LLC, 29
DVIC/NARA/Dreyfuss, cover (middle); NARA/U.S. Navy, 7; PH1 David Miller, 20
Getty Images Inc./Hulton Archive, 10, 18; Joe Munroe, 14; Time Life Pictures/
    Mai/Mai, 16; Time Life Pictures/Photo by U.S. Marine Corps, 17; Time Life
    Pictures/W. Eugene Smith, 25
The Granger Collection, New York, 26
Naval Historical Foundation/NARA/U.S. Navy Photo, cover (top)
Shutterstock/Michael G. Smith, 4

1 2 3 4 5 6 13 12 11 10 09 08

TABLE OF CONTENTS

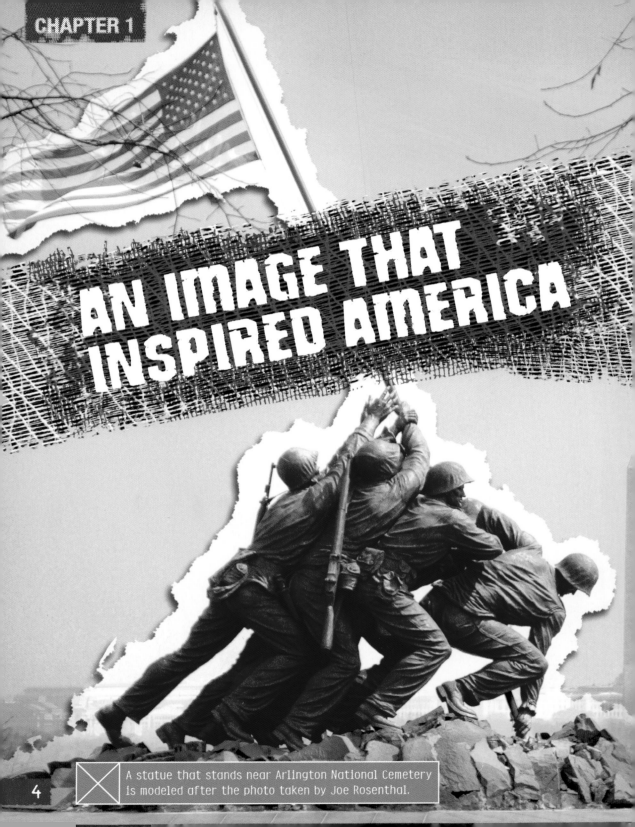

CHAPTER 1

AN IMAGE THAT INSPIRED AMERICA

A statue that stands near Arlington National Cemetery is modeled after the photo taken by Joe Rosenthal.

For four days in 1945, U.S. and Japanese soldiers fought each other on the Pacific island of Iwo Jima. On the fifth morning, February 23, six marines scaled the island's mountain, Mount Suribachi. There, on the highest point of the island, they raised the American flag.

Photographer Joe Rosenthal was on the mountain taking photos for American newspapers. Rosenthal turned around and saw the flag going up. He quickly snapped a few frames. Without knowing it, Rosenthal took a photo that would inspire a nation.

During World War II (1939–1945), the United States and Japan both wanted to control Iwo Jima. Thousands of soldiers died fighting for the island. Americans were upset over the high death toll there. But Rosenthal's photo inspired them. It showed that the United States could win, even with heavy losses. The soldiers had not given up. The flag was a symbol of their fighting spirit.

The U.S. in World War II

On December 7, 1941, Japan attacked the U.S. Naval base at Pearl Harbor, Hawaii. Thousands of Americans died. The United States declared war on Japan the very next day.

The United States joined a group of countries called the Allies. The Allies included Great Britain, France, the Soviet Union, and Canada. The Allies were at war with the countries of Germany, Italy, and Japan. They were called the Axis powers.

The Axis powers had suffered from poor economies. Germany and Italy were also upset about the World War I (1914–1918) peace settlement. They were determined to gain more power and land. The Axis powers built up their militaries and attacked other countries.

FACT:

In about two hours, the Japanese sunk or damaged eight U.S. battleships. They also killed 2,403 Americans and wounded 1,178 more.

During the attack on Pearl Harbor, the Japanese sunk the USS *Arizona*, killing 1,177 American servicemen.

The three surviving men who raised the famous flag on Iwo Jima were treated like celebrities back home.

The Price of Victory

The Battle of Iwo Jima was one of the deadliest battles on the Pacific war front. Almost 7,000 Americans died, and about 20,000 were wounded. More than 20,000 Japanese soldiers lost their lives.

The fate of the men who climbed Mount Suribachi is a good example of the danger of the battle. Forty-one men from a marine platoon secured the mountain for the United States. Only four of them left the island unhurt.

Three of the six men who raised the flag in the famous photo were later killed on the island. They raised the flag on the fifth day of battle. But it took weeks for the fighting to end.

CHAPTER 2

AT WAR WITH JAPAN

While many American men volunteered for military service, American women worked in weapons factories.

Japan had been preparing for war for years. The Japanese had built aircraft carriers, submarines, and battleships. They also had fighter planes and bombers. Some Japanese pilots, called **kamikaze** pilots, flew their airplanes into the Allies' ships, knowing they would die.

The United States had more people and resources than Japan. But the nation was not prepared for war. During the Great Depression (1929–1939), Americans weren't building weapons. They were worried about finding jobs and having enough food to eat.

All that changed when Japan attacked Pearl Harbor. The United States quickly organized its war effort. Young men volunteered to serve in the military. The United States trained soldiers and opened weapons factories. Soon the nation had fighter planes and submarines. It had bombs, machine guns, and rifles. The United States also began developing a new weapon, the **atomic bomb**.

kamikaze — a term used for Japanese pilots who crashed their planes into enemy targets on purpose

atomic bomb — a powerful bomb that explodes with great force and leaves behind dangerous radiation

An Important Island

The United States needed air bases in the Pacific Ocean for its airplanes to land on and refuel. The Allies had captured the South Pacific island of Saipan in June 1944. Now they wanted Iwo Jima. The island would provide an air base for Allied planes making bombing raids on Japan.

The Japanese had already built two airfields on Iwo Jima and had plans for a third. Japanese fighters and bombers could refuel there before attacking Allied ships. The Japanese needed to keep the Americans from taking this air base.

[ASIA]

JAPAN

TOKYO

IWO JIMA

SAIPAN

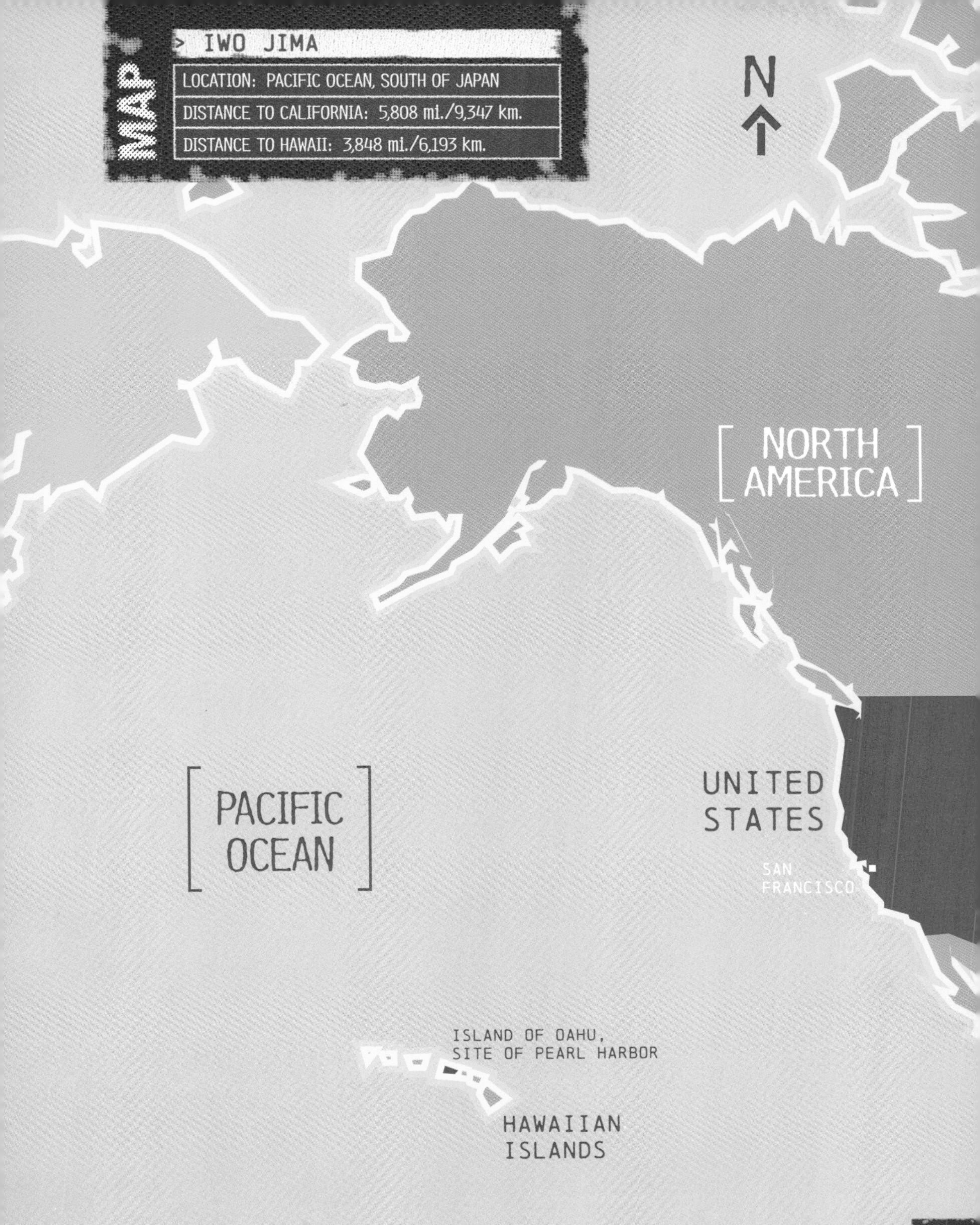

MAP
> IWO JIMA
LOCATION: PACIFIC OCEAN, SOUTH OF JAPAN
DISTANCE TO CALIFORNIA: 5,808 mi./9,347 km.
DISTANCE TO HAWAII: 3,848 mi./6,193 km.
N
NORTH AMERICA
UNITED STATES
SAN FRANCISCO
PACIFIC OCEAN
ISLAND OF OAHU, SITE OF PEARL HARBOR
HAWAIIAN ISLANDS

The skeletons of Japanese soldiers can still be found in the caves of Iwo Jima.

Japanese Preparations

Japanese soldiers arrived on Iwo Jima in the summer of 1944. They prepared to defend against an attack. The Japanese set up machine guns and **artillery** inside Mount Suribachi's caves. They aimed their guns at the beaches. The Japanese also dug miles of tunnels. They hid weapons in caves and tunnels so U.S. soldiers would not see them.

The Japanese built small concrete buildings called pillboxes to hide in. A pillbox had a narrow window to shoot from and a room for weapons and ammunition.

The Japanese also built hidden observation areas where they could watch the American soldiers. They planned to use radios to tell fellow soldiers where to direct attacks.

The Japanese soldiers knew they probably wouldn't win this battle. The United States had far more soldiers. But Japan wanted to make a U.S. victory as difficult as possible. Each Japanese soldier expected to die. But first, he was expected to kill 10 Americans.

artillery — large, powerful guns that are mounted on wheels or tracks

IWO JIMA: MEDAL OF HONOR

Eighty-one Medals of Honor were awarded to soldiers during World War II. This medal is the highest award for bravery. Of the soldiers who fought on Iwo Jima, 27 received the Medal of Honor. Thirteen of these soldiers gave their lives during the battle. American Fleet Admiral Chester W. Nimitz said of the soldiers who fought on Iwo Jima, "Uncommon valor was a common virtue."

U.S. Preparations

U.S. planes bombed Iwo Jima for 72 days before troops went ashore. But the bombing did little to the Japanese soldiers. They were protected in caves and tunnels. The Japanese repaired the bombed airfields on the island, working mainly at night. They held their fire so they wouldn't reveal their positions to the Americans. Finally, U.S. ships began making their way to Iwo Jima. They carried about 80,000 marines who were ready to attack.

Of the U.S. Marines who came ashore on Iwo Jima, one in three was killed or wounded.

17

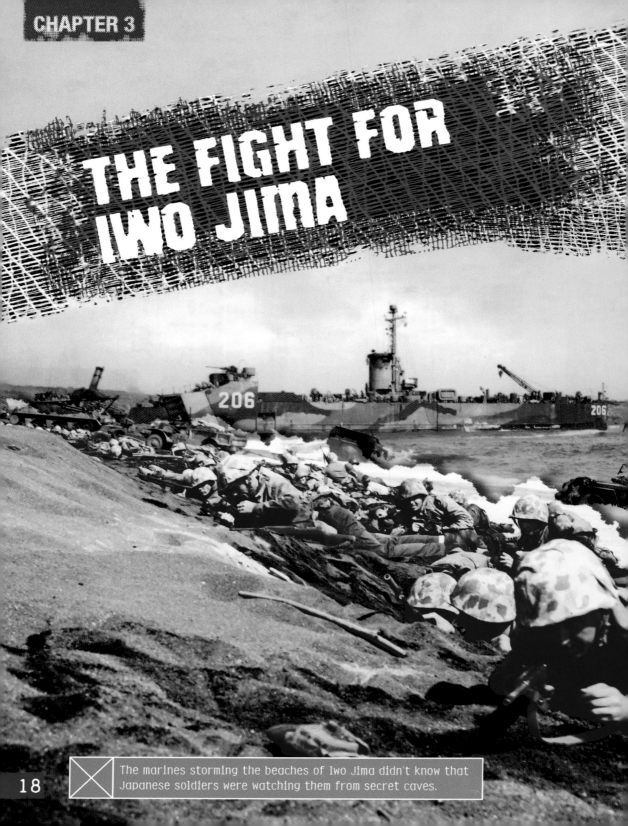

CHAPTER 3

THE FIGHT FOR IWO JIMA

The marines storming the beaches of Iwo Jima didn't know that Japanese soldiers were watching them from secret caves.

The U.S. attack began early on the morning of February 19, 1945. U.S. bombers pounded the island from the air. The boom of firepower tore across the sky. Flashes of light broke through the darkness as mortar shells showered the island. When the sun finally rose, smoke and ash filled the air.

The first wave of marines hit the beaches at 9:00 in the morning. They trudged through sand, slowly making their way toward the airfields. They met little resistance from Japanese troops.

More waves of marines began unloading vehicles and supplies. The sand slowed everything down. Men waded through it, sinking up to their thighs. Vehicles got stuck.

Suddenly, light flashed from Mount Suribachi. Japanese soldiers sent artillery shells flying toward the beach. Japanese machine gunners were hiding near the beach. They opened fire on the marines.

Marines continued wading through the sand, while artillery shells exploded and bullets flew around them. They fell forward and crawled across the earth. Hundreds died, and hundreds more were wounded. Blood soaked the sand. But the marines pressed forward, crawling past the bodies of the dead.

On the day of the invasion, more than 500 marines were killed, and 1,700 were wounded. And it was only the first day of a month-long battle.

A monument stands on top of Mount Suribachi marking the spot where the marines raised the American flag.

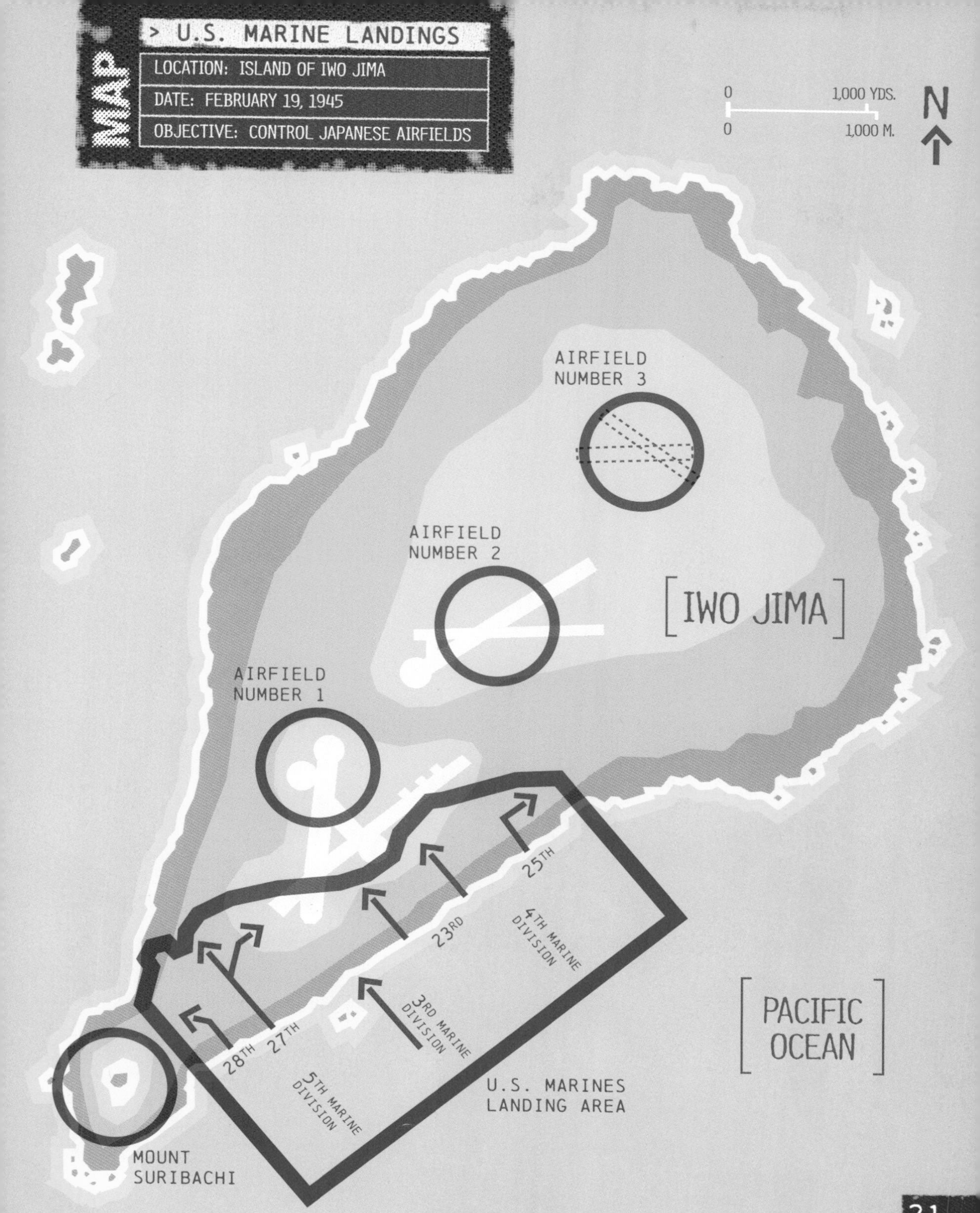
MAP
> U.S. MARINE LANDINGS
LOCATION: ISLAND OF IWO JIMA
DATE: FEBRUARY 19, 1945
OBJECTIVE: CONTROL JAPANESE AIRFIELDS
0
1,000 YDS.
0
1,000 M.
N
AIRFIELD NUMBER 3
AIRFIELD NUMBER 2
[IWO JIMA]
AIRFIELD NUMBER 1
25TH
23RD
4TH MARINE DIVISION
3RD MARINE DIVISION
28TH
27TH
5TH MARINE DIVISION
[PACIFIC OCEAN]
U.S. MARINES LANDING AREA
MOUNT SURIBACHI

Marine photographer Sergeant Lou Lowery took the photo of the first flag raising, just before dodging an enemy grenade.

> THE FIRST FLAG

FACT: The flag in Joe Rosenthal's famous photo was actually a replacement flag. The first flag raised was smaller.

Capturing Mount Suribachi

The island of Iwo Jima was only 8 square miles (21 square kilometers) in size. It had a mountain on one end and airfields along its middle section. The United States wanted to take control of two key points — the mountain and the airfields.

Four days after the invasion, a marine patrol scouted the island's mountain. They were surprised to meet no resistance. A large group of soldiers followed them up the mountain. A few of the soldiers tied an American flag to a pole and raised it at 10:30 in the morning.

The flag could be seen from the ships in the Pacific and by the soldiers below the mountain. U.S. soldiers cheered, and the ships blew their whistles. It was a proud moment. After days of fighting, the United States had taken the high ground.

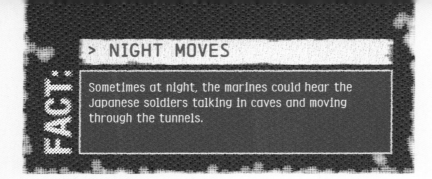

> NIGHT MOVES

Sometimes at night, the marines could hear the Japanese soldiers talking in caves and moving through the tunnels.

Pressing Forward

After the mountain was captured, Japanese soldiers could not shoot down at U.S. troops. The U.S. soldiers could see where the Japanese were firing from. They could tell the crewmen on the U.S. Navy ships where to aim their guns.

The fighting was far from over, though. Many Japanese soldiers were still on the island in hidden tunnels. The marines needed to find these enemy soldiers. They also had to destroy the Japanese pillboxes and find the **snipers**. The marines used **flamethrowers** to kill the Japanese soldiers inside the caves and pillboxes. They continued to attack the Japanese with machine guns, rifles, and grenades.

Finally, on March 26, the United States declared that the island had been secured. But the nation paid a heavy price. More than 26,000 American soldiers were killed or wounded. About 20,000 Japanese soldiers died in the battle.

sniper — a soldier trained to shoot at long-distance targets
flamethrower — a weapon that shoots burning liquid

In addition to flamethrowers, marines used
explosives to destroy Japanese caves and pillboxes.

CHAPTER 4

AN END TO THE WAR

On August 14, 1945, Americans celebrated the news of Japan's surrender to the Allies.

After capturing Iwo Jima, the United States had a new landing base for its airplanes. Before World War II ended, 2,400 B-29 bombers found safety there.

The United States continued to slowly move toward Japan. The next island the Allies overtook was Okinawa, about 350 miles (563 kilometers) south of Japan.

The Allies wanted to end the war as quickly as possible. The United States had finished work on the powerful atomic bomb. The bomb was successfully tested in July 1945. The Allies tried to make a peace settlement, but Japan refused. On August 6, 1945, the United States dropped an atomic bomb on Hiroshima. On August 9, another bomb was dropped on Nagasaki. More than 140,000 people were killed in the attacks, and thousands more died later from radiation poisoning.

Japan's leaders realized they could not win against such powerful weapons. Japan accepted the Allies' terms for surrender on August 14, 1945. Japan did not officially surrender until September 2, 1945.

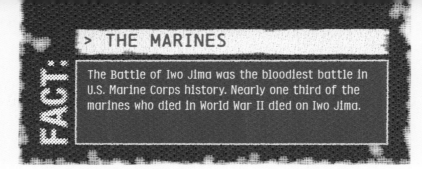
An Inspiring Victory

The photo taken on Iwo Jima still inspires people. It shows that when Americans work together, they can achieve great things. When the photo was taken, thousands of U.S. soldiers were dying. Americans at home were getting tired of the war. The photo helped convince the nation that the sacrifices were worth it.

Victory on Iwo Jima was an important step toward ending World War II. It allowed the Allies to continue to press toward Japan. The Allied victory in World War II ended the violence. But the war's bloody battles left a lasting mark on the world.

7th WAR LOAN NOW··ALL TOGETHER

The photo of the flag raising was used on posters to help promote war loans.

GLOSSARY

Allies (a-LYZ) — a group of countries that fought together in World War II; the Allies included Great Britain, France, and the United States.

artillery (ar-TIL-uh-ree) — cannons and other large guns used during battles

atomic bomb (uh-TOM-ik BOM) — a powerful bomb that explodes with great force, heat, and bright light; atomic bombs destroy large areas and leave behind dangerous radiation.

Axis powers (AK-siss POU-urs) — a group of countries that fought together in World War II; the Axis powers included Japan, Italy, and Germany.

flamethrower (FLAYM-throh-uhr) — a weapon that shoots a stream of burning liquid

kamikaze (kah-mi-KAH-zee) — a Japanese pilot during World War II who would purposely crash his plane into a target, resulting in his own death

pillbox (PIL-boks) — a small, low concrete building; during the battle of Iwo Jima, Japanese soldiers shot machine guns from pillboxes.

sniper (SNY-pur) — a soldier trained to shoot at long-distance targets from a hidden place

READ MORE

Adams, Simon. *World War II.* Eyewitness. New York: DK Publishing, 2004.

Hama, Larry. *The Battle of Iwo Jima: Guerilla Warfare in the Pacific.* Graphic Battles of World War II. New York: Rosen, 2007.

Hama, Larry. *Island of Terror: Battle of Iwo Jima.* Osprey Graphic History. New York: Osprey, 2006.

INTERNET SITES

FactHound offers a safe, fun way to find Internet sites related to this book. All of the sites on FactHound have been researched by our staff.

Here's how:
1. Visit *www.facthound.com*
2. Choose your grade level.
3. Type in this book ID **1429619392** for age-appropriate sites. You may also browse subjects by clicking on letters, or by clicking on pictures and words.
4. Click on the **Fetch It** button.

FactHound will fetch the best sites for you!

INDEX